MISPLACED ORGANS & VARIOUS SAINTS

MISPLACED ORGANS & VARIOUS SAINTS

Poems about love, God & violence

Dante Émile

QUERENCIA

Querencia Press, Chicago IL

QUERENCIA PRESS

© Copyright 2024
Dante Émile

ISBN 978 1 959118 71 8

www.querenciapress.com

First Published in 2024

Querencia Press, LLC
Chicago IL

Printed & Bound in the United States of America

To lovers, past & present.

CONTENTS

a prayer

Maybe if I drop on my knees on the bathroom floor
God will be able to hear me more clearly,

                                                     any words spoken naked must count as prayer.

Do the cracks in my ceiling open up to Heaven?
I swear I can hear angels nesting inside the chimney,

                                        the fluttering of feathers keeps me awake at night.

So here is a list of all of my sins,
sorted by bloodshed & in alphabetical order.
So here are the names of every person I've tried to replace you with,
going from a school teacher to the man that
lent me his lighter outside a bar that one time.
If you hold them against the light you can see the handwriting matches perfectly,
the G & the D curve the same way,

           See? Right there; the O looks a little different but it's just because I was using a different pen.
I've rolled out the carpets & dug up the keys from the garden.
I can attest to every body up in the attic,
they all have my fingerprints & matching scars on their wrists.
I cover them in linen & hope they never get to you.

this love burns you & maims you & twists you inside out

Every day a bullet wound, every day fresh shrapnel to harvest from my chest.

There are four eyes in the mirror & none of them want to look at me,

there are four footprints in the snow & they all stop at the doorway.

> *When I love you I lose myself, & when I don't, I disappear,*
>
> *& I've given up on trying to hate you.*

Slice me open & call it a promise, hold my heart down & call it a slaughter.

If there's blood under your fingernails it means I've won,

if there's blood under your fingernails it means you haven't scrubbed hard enough, &

the stain on your floor will only grow larger.

The line of your teeth speaks of salvation, & I'm greeting God with a double-edged sword.

Stick your spear between my ribs, watch it come out of your back,

& who but I will want to stitch you up now?

Kiss my cheek or split my skull in two,

the outcome is still the same.

dreamhome heartaches

Let me see what dances behind those eyes. Let me set them on the bedside table & scoop your brains out with my fingers. This way we're even. This way we finally have nothing to hide. The way your skin barely holds you together tells me to keep pulling at the seams until it comes down like theatre drapes.

Step into the belly of the beast & find instead land to lay your foundations.

This could be the main bedroom, you could leave your books in here, & right there, on the corner, an oven big enough to fit the both of us.

You stand beside me as the world crumbles for the second time tonight & remind me that destruction & creation were birthed from the same womb, & a God is a God because we allow him to be.

This house I've built in the eye of the storm holds its breath for us.

Shed your masks in the foyer & wait for me inside.

XIII

suburbia judas

Fine, you can have this.

You get to be holy & good, you get flowers on the doorstep & silent *he never really deserved yous*. You get to dump it on the side of the road on moving day, looking behind only to check how far ahead you've gotten already.

Congratulations! You made it! You get to drive the car home, the million-dollar prize, baby. You get the standing ovation & the royalty-free victory tune. Smile for the camera, blow a kiss to the audience, the only way to go from here is up.

What do I get? I get to carry this cross around. I get holes in my shoes & nicotine stains on the walls. Because nothing about what I gave you was real. Because I was only

occupying the space you arranged for me like a tenant

who knows he'll have to pack his bags again come summer.

You wanted something to write about & I served you my lungs on a silver platter.

I will play the part for you, sweetheart, I'll be exactly what you want me to be. I'll be the villain, the monster, the killer. They'll talk about it for years.

He was born for it, they'll say, *he wears it like a second skin.*

So here's what I get:

I get to fire the gun this time. I get a box of matches & a gallon of gasoline. I get the grand honour of being defeated.

Kill the lights, stop recording,

the story has been told.

love of the wolf

The world holds its breath when the lamb opens its jaws,

the wolf falls to its knees.

No greater worship than that of the predator about to be eaten,

                                                         no God like a ravenous prey.

Bare your teeth & I'll bare mine & we can devour our monsters.

The road back home is paved with good intentions,

the road back home is lit with foolish flames.

If we make it there we get to peel the skin off the carcass,

we get to hang the pelts by the door,

but the woods are cruel & endless, yes,

                            & so are we.

& the first thing we must survive is each other.

two boys, in embrace

We know about shame, you & I, we have left it at the doorway.

I wrote you a song only the sky will hear. You told me

everything looks better in the middle of the night & under a weak bedside lamp.

When I hand you my naked body, I'm asking for nothing more

than for you to put it in its place. I humble myself by praying

you decide to spend some spare time with it. Your teeth on my shoulder

a reminder that nothing good comes out of pleasure.

If God knows of the things we do behind closed doors, he's got a raging hard-on.

If God cares he's leaving open-mouthed kisses on both of our crooked spines.

The room is bathed in light which means we are still alive. Which means we are somewhere underwater. Lungs

flood and I'm right there where you want me, gasping against your thigh & hoping this is what finally kills me.

Tell me you love me & I will ruin this for the both of us,

       tell me you love me & I will crash this car into the first lamplight I come across.

See I'm not too good with ghosts & even worse with skeletons. There is something about the way the bones rattle every time I open the bedroom door, sardonic laughter mixed with the steady rhythm of a homecoming tune.

So let's talk about something else, yeah?

Like maybe the way the moon highlights the arch of your lips, or how I can only explain the state of my mind by stealing somebody else's words.

I was never good at heart-to-hearts—can I borrow a cigarette? Sleep in your bed? Eat out of your palm? Fuck your friends? Bleed myself dry on your kitchen floor?

I promise to clean up after myself, & you can finally answer the question on everybody's mind:

how does it feel with both hands around my throat?

Or better yet, you can lie & say it has nothing to do with the way our bodies slot together.

Up to you. I'll be waiting.

(untitled)

I swallow my tongue alongside sleeping pills so I can stop myself from asking

if you still love me for the third time this week.

Believe me, darling, if I had anything else to offer aside from this

poorly stitched heart I would hand it to you.

In a dream, I put my head on your lap & you let me cry until there's nothing left of me.

In a dream, I'm on my knees & unforgivable.

There's this one where you don't exist & I keep tearing pages out of a handbook.

That's the one I wake up shaking from.

      There are about a hundred things I don't tell you & a hundred things I don't tell myself,

& most of the time I'm just scared, worried you might wander off to the room I always try to keep locked &

decide you don't wanna live here anymore.

One of my faces wants to say *here you go, here's the key, have a look around. There's a chest next to the haunted*

dolls with every version of me I've tried to drown on the inside.

Now help me make a choice.

I will drag this out in the open, but you have to tell me there's still some road ahead of us.

I will keep walking if you just keep talking, & hope we never get to see the end of it.

a car-crash

Light shoots out of me with the same rage rats crawl around my shadow, so it's up to you—
either you end up blinding yourself or cleaning up teeth-shaped wounds in a rest-stop bathroom.
One way or another the car crashes & I'm in the middle of the street yelling,
hit me, hit me & you will know how it feels to live in here.
Chewing out my leg like a wild animal so I can get the hell out before it catches me.
But the headlights are always faster & the roads never change,
& I've been in this place long enough to know you can never escape a self-imposed villain,
sooner or later the brakes fail,
or there's a deer head in your windshield,
& the car always always always always always crashes.

monster theory

When do we become so rotten the earth won't even take us back?
What is it that will finally force us to strip from our cloaks of humanity?
What makes me terrible, truly? The fire or what I choose to do with it?

Is this a monster? This version of me, now,
branding every word I write like a gutting knife?
When I dream of slicing you open & crawling inside you
of making a place where I can finally fit?
When I wake up & turn around to tell you?

What *is* a monster?
It's what slips through the cracks in my voice, it's the pill I can't seem to swallow,
screaming *take me as I am or kill me*
screaming *peel my skin off like a blindfold*
screaming *love me despite the horror*
screaming *please, God, love me because of it.*

love song of two vampires

I say I see you & you say bite

the tender flesh on the inside of my wrist. Drink

from the fountain of my obscenity until you're satisfied.

I have covered my skin in solitude

for way too long. Want to strip down to my very bones, now.

Want to dance to the sound of your pulse against my lips, now.

      Newborn

      nakedness & well-loved blood.

The only thing a monster needs

is another one like him. Do you understand? The only thing

a monster needs is a big open book & a warm place to haunt.

Teach me how to hold the night sky like a diamond between my teeth,

how to walk this town unafraid of the footsteps in the mud. Tomb

to tomb in the nooks & crannies of your life. Make room for me

on the left side of your burial shroud.

Love,

die with me this once

& you will understand what the earth can give

to the unbridled one.

a ritual

He's not empty, he's been hollowed out.

All the discarded pieces tossed in a makeshift funeral pyre at the foot of his bed.

If you were to press your face to his body you could almost make the other side of it.

There is something wrong with how he's made. Something about the way he stares at the space between his words. How his hands always seem to flutter like wounded doves about to take flight.

A man is a man is a man no matter how the word echoes in your ribcage.

A girl is a girl is a girl who doesn't care how many times you've buried her.

For every bit of himself, there is about a pound of someone else:

Striking vision of his father, lousy resolution of his mother.

Eternal not-himself.

Eternal clouded mirror.

a city

I don't know how to keep it all inside,
love pouring out like light between the leaves.
The trees, my ribs, You, the streetlamp.
Love like a letter you never finish writing, like
a cathedral in the centre of the universe.
Love like the sun setting on the arches of a new city.
I build this place around your voice,
every narrow street, a vein I've left open,
a monument for every time you've held my heart against the pavement.
A canal for all of it to wash away
forget it, my dear, it's already in the ocean.
Come visit sometime.

about the eternal resentment of being put together

Wounded doves in the kitchen sink.

Blood-stained white wings.

Wolves that bite but don't break skin.

I hold all of these to my chest so I might ask you about it later.

There is something to be said about dreams & prophecies,

something about dogs chasing their own tails.

      I tell my mother I hate her the way every kid hates their mom,

viciously & against my will. My father doesn't answer when I ask,

but the kitchen is empty & there are feathers between his teeth.

Everything ends up getting swallowed & I'm never fast enough to catch it in mid-flight.

      In this world of my own, I curl up on the supermarket floor & sob like a newborn. In this world of

my own, I make everyone complicit in my grief.

      Here is my heart, which is a fist, which is a candle, which is an apple left to rot on the dining table.

      I ask the wolves to bite harder,

please let there be a remnant of your teeth,

at least while I'm in here,

but they wag their tails, & hold me by the throat,

& I have never known gentleness that wouldn't end in blood.

new years' eve

Drinking red wine out of coffee mugs & reinventing what it means
to believe in something. Finding religion inside broken pieces of glass,
counting the knots in your spine like beads from a holy rosary.
Holy headlights, drunken praise, bruised knees for all the wrong reasons.
I sing these psalms in candle-lit chapels & pray to the saints of your body.

a conversation with william s. burroughs

"Death is only waiting for something to begin,"

late beat poet William S. Burroughs told me in a dream.

Sitting in front of me, somber as the grave he's held in, a long table spread between us,

& a vase of withered daisies as a centerpiece.

"Why did you kill your wife?" I ask him.

Next to him sits a man who is not a man with a face that's not quite a face.

"The bullet was always in her, I simply aimed at temptation."

The man who is not a man has bees in his eyes & swallows bible pages.

Take off the grave clothes & let him go.

I tell him: "Bullshit. You should've gone to jail."

He tells me: "Stop forcing coffins open."

He tells me: "Who among us doesn't have blood on their hands."

The tombs were open & the saints who had fallen asleep were raised.

The face that is not a face is crying a rainforest.

In front of me, a bowl filled with baby teeth.

"The only blood I've spilled has been my own."

"A murder of the self is still a murder," his glasses turn to mirrors. "& perhaps that's why you're here. To get an alibi."

"No one believes a ghost."

"Then you should run & tell them," the man who is not a man says, with a mouth that is not a mouth, "before they forget how your voice sounds."

XXVI

a wound

      God, I do think my hands were made to carry your burdens,

I fill them up with water from my stream & bring them to your lips.

A wound is a door is a window is the space where you & I can finally touch.

I crawl into you through the scar on your side & set camp,

light my candles, put my prayers down.

Will you love me now? With my insides tangled up with yours? Am I forgiven?

I see my life through the holes in your palms & nail it to a tree.

If you hear me, you're not listening. If you're listening, you don't care.

      Render my soul obsolete & grant me another,

let it tear at my skin like a crown of thorns,

let me make it worth the stay.

personal theology

Let my words be naked or let there be none. Let me take faith in my arms & break it.

I've been trying to remember how it feels to believe in something, to look up at the sky & see more than darkness.
It's been hard, you see, I always link up the stars back to you.

        I've been thinking about God which in turn means I've been thinking about You.

(I've been thinking I would like to kill him. I would like to see the way his muscles move, I would have him flayed, open & vulnerable. I think I would like to swallow him up & spit his bird-like frail little bones. I think I would like to fuck him, I think I would like to make him cry.
I think I would love to love him. I think I would love it if he loved me.)

        There is God, & there is You, & there is the space between God & You I only visit with closed eyes.
I try not to think about it, let alone write it.
Scared my words might ricochet back to me once I shoot them.
When I picture you now it's always the back of your head. When I think of you now you're faceless & beautiful & so goddamn cruel.

        I've been thinking I would like it if you finally killed me, I think I could finally rest.
Will you do me this last favour? Take this knife to my chest?
Open up my lungs so I can breathe?
I always did love you to the blissful point of Death.

something in the way the stars look tonight

Something in the way the stars look tonight makes me think we'll be forgiven,

God will hold us in his hands like water & we will travel through his body as children.

Leave your hearts under the floorboards, there is no use for them now.

Blood only sings if you listen to it & there is enough noise to drown it out.

There is music, there is dancing & laughing & socked feet on the carpet.

        Can't you bury your dead where you found them?

Just for tonight, can we pretend the cracks in our souls have been filled with melted gold?

That our churches aren't in ruins & we only scream because there is so much to be said?

That what hangs from our ceiling is not a rope but a chandelier?

a story

        Here's how the story goes:

I tell you I love you & you tell me there will always be someone else sleeping in my bed. I tell you *Listen, I can carve in a place for you. I can buy a new mattress. I can sleep on the floor. I can sell all my stuff & move to Madrid, & God knows I hate Madrid.*

So there's a body under my sheets, big fucking deal; it's not like your slate is clean. We both have stories to bury & none of us really know how deep we should dig. The dog keeps bringing the bones back home: he wants to play with our dead, he wants us to toss them just to see them come back again.

        & here's how the story goes: I say there is nothing I wouldn't do for you & you say there is nothing to be done, anyway. You say, *You don't understand, I cannot carry the weight of your heart. I cannot carry it with me, it's too much.*

So I'll throw it away, I will leave it behind, & I will offer the hole in my chest to whoever is in need of a place to land. Now neither of us can have it, see. It's gone. Good job. Good luck. Goodbye. Let's move on. It's been a year & I'm still waiting for that night to burn.

        & here's how the story goes: everything ends up under the cathedral stones, everything ends up right where you left it,

& I cannot walk past the old town without it tugging at my clothes.

XXX

a dream

I am not done talking about Dreams.

The way birds hang on my eyelids like telephone wire, whisper half-eaten conversations about long-lost friends, about sorrow.

The way Walt Whitman takes me gently by the arm,

shows me the rich green field and says:

So much beauty. So much beauty everywhere and you can't stop looking at your hands.

I am not done talking about Death,

how it seems to always find its way back to me. Speaks like an old friend and holds me like a lover. Wax-sealed notes and roses. A housewarming party.

Remember the shape of the wolf's teeth, remember the sound of breaking skin:

This is my God; this is how He speaks.

a vision

God came to me today,

like a ghost, like a whisper.

He flew in through my open window,

pressed His body against mine & said:

You will find yourself at the throat of love again.

Rejoice. Despair.

You have not been swallowed yet.

a prayer (II)

1.

God opens my body up & feasts from it.

Slithers through the gaps in my conscience like a plague.

God-ridden. God-infected.

2.

He swallows me up & spits me out again; my soul made of apple seeds, his mouth falling over me like locusts,

sword buried to the darkest parts of me. Light pouring through the holes in my palms like moonbeams.

Holy light, holy darkness, holy absence of revelation.

3.

Hunger leaving marks on my body, sickly cues of divinity.

Gospel made flesh, flesh made word, naked feet striking the earth like thunder.

God-hollow. God-starving.

4.

Running around in circles trying to catch a glimpse of your face.

The branches of the olive trees casting countless shadows on my skin.

If you call I will answer, but first, you must call.

Holy voice, holy silence, holy ringing in my ears.

the last supper

He has never looked more beautiful. The purple light cuts bodies down like a chisel. Makes God out of every corner lips go to die. / He opens his arms to welcome you & you understand why they call him the saviour. Forget the fishes, forget the bread; his dilated pupils are miracle enough. / You never asked for holiness, you just wanted to know how his teeth would feel on your neck. / The boys in the bathroom sing psalms between lines of coke, hold each other's hands & yell, *He's healed! He's healed!* & what can you do, really, but believe them. / Hips to hips, dust to dust. / His mouth the gates of paradise, his tongue a flood upon your brick house. / Tomorrow when they take him, he will not remember this moment, but you will. / Tomorrow when they take him, he will have nothing but a headache & a lipstick stain on his cheek. / But tonight he laughs as he spins you around, dances to a beat only he can feel, and you don't understand why you were chosen to do this. / God if you're listening let this cup pass from me, let me have another shot instead.

john sleeps

John sleeps.

He's the youngest, the sweetest, the one who picks up flowers to put them in your hair, who joins in every time Mary starts to sing, who kisses the back of your ear when you're stressed.

He's also the one who drinks too much wine very early in the evening & passes out accordingly. & hey, you say, it happens. He looks at you with half-lidded eyes & a lopsided smile. He's tired, he says, & you put a hand on his forehead & let him go. The remaining eleven apostles will tease him mercilessly once he wakes, but for now, they're too busy passing bottles of wine around.

Before God took him by the hand this cherub-faced fisherman would spend the hours down the dock with his father. Sunrise to dawn, the sun hitting his naked back, turning soft skin into gold. Sharing with his brother jokes only they could understand. Calloused hands where there should only be gentleness. But then again, only time for resting was time for prayer, & you swear you can see him: fresh-faced & even younger, on his knees asking for his neighbours to have something to eat that day, for the ache in his father's back to diminish, for his brother to sleep soundly for one night.

The wind makes the curls on his head dance, & there's a phantom ache somewhere inside you, a divine calling to let your fingers card through them. Wake him up. Ask him to pray with you. Kiss the palm of his hands. Rest your head on his shoulder.

There are so many things a body can do when it loves. So many things this skin will long for once it is all done.

XXXV

Tonight the light disappears down the garden, as it always does. Tonight you get to carve the edge of his nose for the last time. Tonight, alone & frightened, you have nothing but the memories of warm bodies against your own, & it should be enough. The soft caress of a memory, it should be enough.

Tonight, that you know will be the last night. He's there, peaceful & beautiful.

It should be enough. It isn't.

But you know that, just like the rest of you, he doesn't get to sleep much these days.

John sleeps, & you let him. Your only wish that God doesn't wake him before you're gone.

gethsemane

What did you think about,
while the others slept? When the silence was total except for
one or two insomniac birds. Did you think of your father?
The other one,
the one with calloused hands and sawdust in his beard. The one who
sang you to sleep when you had a fever. Did you remember
the sea, the little fishes at your feet?
How they seemed to know it all about
divinity. How little they cared about it.
Did you think of your mother and how she held moonlight in her eyes? How she
washed your hair by the river and taught you the meaning of Grace?
The sun sets over the garden and you
weep. The light does not look like that from up above.
Did you perhaps look back at him,
peaceful, quiet, his lips slightly parted as he dreams, and said:
This I will miss.
The rise and fall of the chest, the
flutter of eyelashes against your cheek, the taste of wine on
somebody else's tongue. The body as God's vessel for
pleasure. For love.
Did you see the silver, the rope hanging from the tree, and, through tears,
whisper a prayer for him too?

XXXVII

after abel

Two brothers in a field are enough for the tragedy to start.

The Lord says, *bring me something worthwhile,* & the boy puts his hands to task.

       Mother used to say

I had a gift for it. I was my father's son, I envied the way flowers bloomed.

Cain takes a swig at his vodka & tonic & shows you the scar on his forehead.

He tells you he's picked up some Spanish in his travels, signals to the waiter & says,

me & my brother, you see, we were uña y carne.

This is what happens when God slips between two sleeping bodies,

       he ruins them.

Who kills their own brother?

       Well,

someone who loves him very much.

He makes of womb

an altar & prays,

I have shed for you

the truth of life. Could you please

bring him back?

Abel was the slaughterer, I only watered the plants.

He orders another drink. *God wants blood,* he says,

blood & regret. So I handed him my heart.

XXXVIII

When they were little Cain would sit on the porch & listen to the trees grow.

Something about the quietness of creation.

When you love a lamb,

you hold its neck while you bleed it.

Cain raises his arm & pleads:

Close your eyes.

do angels exist? or a google search a week off antipsychotics

Do angels exist?

I once mistook one for a pigeon, the fluttering of flight was the same. It had one bad leg & was dragging behind one of its wings. *Nothing to do about that one,* said my father, so we left it to aimlessly roam the city streets. This place is no place for an angel, I thought, but would anything have changed had I nursed you back to health?

Do angels have gender?

Or do they, like me, rejoice in the playground of human concoctions? Saint Michael puts on a skirt before going out & twirls. Somewhere a young trans body is enveloped by the blessing of a summer breeze. Somewhere a young trans body finally gets to know what it means when people say grace.

Do angels have free will?

A cherub blows cigarette smoke out all three of their mouths, prays the Father never finds out. Later that night, they will sneak out the window & lose their shoes in a punk show where they will mosh with one of the fallen. A seraph gets lost in the sheets of some moon-eyed man, his wings ruffled by the dance of human sin. He will tell no one but will hold the memory of the man's skin like a pot of gold.

Do angels have wings?

Do they use them to cover each other's halos when it starts to rain? Do they share wings like children share blankets & wait for it all to end? Every leaf I've ever found on the ground has been proof of a miracle. Every piece of holiness is a rock I've kept hidden in my pocket. God is the size of an apple heart & weighs about 70 kilograms or as much as a feather, depending on who you ask.

Do angels have souls?

& do they ache as ours do? Do they carry them like hearses everywhere they go? I always thought the soul was a burden until somebody held it in their hands.

Do angels sit on your bed?

Or are they just the only light left by my window after the last star has gone out? The remaining spot of clarity under the oxidising night; a candle burning at both ends; an old friend calling, frantically saying *pick it up, pick it up, pick it up.*

Do angels sing?

& if they do, do they take requests? I was thinking of some Chet Baker to start with, something slow & sweet to soothe the wandering soul. *My funny valentine / sweet comic valentine / you make me smile with my heart.* I hope Heaven is full of jazz, full of trumpets & sad voices, I hope a certain level of melancholy is allowed. The body needs some grief to survive.

Do angels sleep?

They must dream, at least.

Goodnight.

king solomon splits my heart in two

There is a rhythm to these things. The birds & the voices,

they don't come all at once. The magpie knows when she needs to be heard, so does God.

Yesterday I prayed for a miracle, today I'm finding feathers everywhere.

      The bird says *what do you think will happen after I'm dead?* It's an odd

question to ask. Nine words. Two lifetimes. It should be enough.

What do I think? Easy. I think he will never stop loving you, & neither will I,

& one of us will have to carry the sword back home.

      The bird says *which part of me gets to claim this victory?* & I tell him

whichever has the guts left to do it.

      Sparrow-hearted boy, the only thing you have to fear is yourself.

Collect your wings, say your goodbyes. The world does not wait for you.

true love is kept in a shoebox under your bed

The birth of a year bites ferociously.
I claw January's eyes out with my nails &
pray February brings me more than adulthood.
I don't think I'm ready to be grown.
Not quite ready for box-of-matches winters &
flickering-light-bulb summers.
There is a song at the edge of the world you only know the first verses of.
Finish singing it & Death will drop at your feet and ask for forgiveness.
Old lovers haunt me like a thousand fruit flies,
paper thin wings of angels circling my
rotten peach head.
I sink my teeth into other people's tragedies,
sleep too much & get accustomed to an absence of
call it touch
call it love.
Us four sat on the floor when you tell me
true love
is kept in a shoebox under your bed.

XLIII

No other reason for me to keep holding on to his handwriting.

Always loved the way his *I* curved, the way ink spilled like blood splatter.

Never knew how he managed to make wound out of word.

I light my cigarette in the sacrificial fire of

your memory & swallow every cloud of smoke.

      Who knows,

maybe one day I'll get used to it.

holy week

Like any naked animal I only know what I am if I'm on my knees begging for it.

      Empty coffee mugs & songs about cities you will never get to visit

fill you up like a pitcher of water balanced on God's greying head.

Strangers you could grow to love if only you got rid of the body down in your basement.

The filth of the old town paints a picture only you seem to be able to see.

      The boy with the crooked smile tells you he likes your coat &

you dream of melting butter inside his mouth. Your fingers

reach for his hair as the gin sets heavy on your tongue. Liquid foolishness mixed with the need to tear at a man's

pulse with your rotten teeth.

Stare at the ashes of borrowed cigarettes when he leaves the party with someone else.

The sickly-sweet taste of loneliness when they tell you, you will always be their friend. Try not to get lost in the

thought of *maybe someday.*

      Boys like you can't afford butterflies—boys like you get stab wounds.

Boys like you carry their body on their shoulders

like in *Semana Santa*, but boys like you don't get to kiss the Virgin's knees.

Absolution stings like alcohol for boys like you. You can take it or leave it,

but the burnt shape of lips on the back of your hand

will be there every time you look at it.

antigone of the south

Swarms of angels circle my ripe apple-heart.
Moth to a flame,
match to the skin, cardinal red.
I wear my cloak-like grief
draped around my shoulders.
I carry the screams of my dead
like a wooden cross. Splinters of recognition
under every single one of my nails. Chorus of
old gods narrating the tragedy of my survival.
A vault brimming with all the gold they promised to give back &
a half-buried brother. Antigone of the South.
Blood on my hands, on their hands, on your hands,
& not a single drop of rain anywhere.

psalm

Bless me. Bless me. Bless me.
There is something about the
rain. Something about
rainbows on the pavement.
It turns my heart into a waterfall,
makes me want to fall to my knees
and pray. I hide between journal
pages, I drown in cups of coffee,
I wonder how other people do it.
Life, I mean. I don't know how to
handle it. Does everyone feel like
they're leaving a piece of themselves
behind every time they say *I miss you*?
Bless me. Bless me. Bless me. Bless me.
God, I do want more of it. I do. I just have
no place left to store it. The angel puts
their hands on my chest & yells DO
YOU UNDERSTAND? CAN YOU
HEAR THE SONG OF FALLEN
LEAVES? THE WAY SPRING
DANCES JUST BEFORE IT'S
ABOUT TO BREAK?

The rainforest
of my throat says *I don't know*
what it is that opens & closes.
I don't know how to hold onto a
match without burning. Believe in
one thing & the rest will follow.
It's a leap of faith, a drunk walk
home. Set yourself on fire
first thing in the morning
& it will keep you warm all day.
Stuff your mouth with feathers &
try not to choke on the miracle.
My father's shoes in the doorway,
the scent of damp earth. It all
comes back to light, or rather the
absence of it. It all ends up covered
in dust. Haunted houses you once
called home, ghosts you used to call
baby, darling, beloved. My angel-
heart. My applejack. I'm leaving with
more flesh than I can carry. I'm leaving
with all of this behind.
Bless Me. Bless me. Bless me.

portrait of a dream with an open doorway

Perhaps our bodies together would be too good of a thing to last.
        Your little angel bones too fragile for my wandering hands,

your knees unripe, unbruised;
        your wrists the only floodgate in a river of what-if-we-tried.

But I'm greedy, yes, & I'm hungry, &
        the devouring mouth would take hold of this dance in an instant.

So let's leave it like it is, then. Me the dragon & the castle,
        you the princess & the prince.

Or better yet, let's erase this fairytale from both of our libraries. Strip
        the page naked of anything remotely resembling a dream I had about you.

        I'm too used to desire, & not that much at being touched.

You spend so much time behind a moat you start to believe
        bridges are not a thing people build anymore.

XLIX

You spend so much time with your own body you forget
            what the back of a tooth feels like.

Little thing, love would destroy us if given the chance,
            our mouths together like a house on fire, a burnt-down childhood room.

so let's keep our loose lips to ourselves, &
            continue looking for each other in kinder places.

L

the poet as an autopsy table

Break the bones on every finger to point to the sky, & now what? / Nothing has really changed. / It's still the sky, it's still your finger, & you're still dead. / Outside the world keeps its steady pace. / There is no choir, no fanfare, only silence where your voice used to be. / Someone is taking you down to a basement where they will weigh out your sins, / someone is mapping your body just like a lover would. / They undressed you before you came here; your saint lies forgotten somewhere in your grandmother's house, / he will tell everyone to wait for you upstate. / The surgeon makes a note of every scar you've grown up with, everything you could've ever written about that stays inside your wire-shut mouth. / No use explaining old hurts, / now. White-eyed prince, winter boy— / you'd run hot with shame if you could. / Opening up the chest cavity reveals nothing but a worn-out mass / of muscle you used to call your heart, / under it is a lump the size of a walnut you kept your grief in. / Some things you love once & spend the rest of your life pouring salt in the wound. / Some things you love once & spend the rest of your life scrubbing blood stains off the floor. / Forget about poetry, the last thing your body will write / is a coroner's report.

i don't know where my body ends & the anger begins

I don't know where my body ends & the anger begins.

The battleground of my chest yearns for a Christmas miracle, a handshake in no man's land.

Manhood in a vial is not enough to trick people into believing I deserve to be loved, but it will have to do. Bruises on my knees speak of long nights praying for something bigger than myself to rise up from the ground.

There are many of us. All these voices yelling up to Heaven asking for our skin to break in all the right places. For someone to come over and tell us

there is nothing wrong in the way your naked body curves, in how your voice breaks when it drops to your feet.

We're just asking for the doors to be left open for once.

We are running out of bobby pins & our hands are getting numb.

Some of us lose fingers, & that's fair enough. Some of us lose the whole arm.

Some of us have nothing left to lose anymore.

There are many of us.

Enough to build a wall tall enough to keep the rest of the noise out. The buzzing of flies that spell d i r t y on the sky, that swarm the rooms where we huddle up to rest.

The transubstantiation of our blood will render all of these giants obsolete one day.

Will take their bloated pointed fingers & turn them against themselves.

There are many of us,

& we hold each other like twins in a womb. We sharpen our teeth against doctor's reports, against law bills & God's open palms. We dig our death out & hold them up for the world to see.

We say,

here's our soul & our mangled throat, here's what you never will bury.

(untitled)

The boy by the window tells you he will never stop loving you,

& you believe him.

Three months later you're pulling out broken pieces of stained glass from the palms of your hands while he

smokes his lavender cigarette five cities away,

& there are no words in the English language

that quite explain the state of your heart.

Try your luck with a dictionary. Like shortage

of breath when he laced his fingers with yours or clothes,

his & yours, mixed up on the bedroom floor. The way

we undressed to simply lay next to each other.

Sleeping forehead to forehead just to feel him breathing,

& knowing all too well that losing him is the best thing you'll ever do.

on faded polaroids & cigarette ash

I have built you up inside my chest,
       there is a niche in the middle of it where you could fit perfectly
if you dared to step inside.
My doctor shoves a couple of pills down my throat, tells me to swallow.
Says this will get rid of the hole in my skull.
But I want it, it's mine.   It's mine.
(I don't get to claim victory, big deal,
but I get to claim the gaps between your teeth).
The red scar of your city,
       the open wound of your hand on mine.
Is it so bad?
That I still want us to share the same moon? That sometimes
I sit outside & wonder if you're smoking on the windowsill
like we used to do? Sharing lung cancer like
kisses & whispering we're young,
we're still young,
thinking that the world will wait for us?
Is it really so bad,
to have loved?

LV

acknowledgements

Antigone of the South has been published in Defunkt Magazine.

Monster Theory, Dreamhome Heartaches, this love burns you & maims you & twists you inside out and *A Conversation with William S. Burroughs* have been published in Not Deer Magazine

notes

'This Love Burns You & Maims You & Turns You Inside Out' takes its title from Guillermo del Toro's *Crimson Peak.*

'Love of the Wolf' is titled after Hélène Cixous' essay *Love of the Wolf.*

'A Conversation with William S. Burroughs' quotes John 11:44 & Matthew 27:52.

www.ingramcontent.com/pod-product-compliance
Lightning Source LLC
Chambersburg PA
CBHW081341120626
46546CB00011B/3439